A Fine Fat Pig
and other
animal poems

by Mary Ann Hoberman

paintings by Malcah Zeldis

HarperCollins*Publishers*

FRANKLIN PIERCE
COLLEGE LIBRARY
RINDGE, N. H. 03461

A Fine Fat Pig
and other animal poems
Text copyright © 1991 by Mary Ann Hoberman
Illustrations copyright © 1991 by Malcah Zeldis
Printed in the U.S.A. All rights reserved.
1 2 3 4 5 6 7 8 9 10
First Edition

Library of Congress Cataloging-in-Publication Data
Hoberman, Mary Ann.
  A fine fat pig and other animal poems / by Mary Ann Hoberman ;
paintings by Malcah Zeldis.
      p.   cm.
  Summary: Fourteen animal poems include such titles as "Yoo Hoo,
Mrs. Kangaroo" and "One Half of the Giraffe."
  ISBN 0-06-022425-8. — ISBN 0-06-022426-6 (lib. bdg.)
  1. Animals—Juvenile poetry.   2. Children's poetry, American.
[1. Animals—Poetry.   2. American poetry.]   I. Zeldis, Malcah, ill.
II. Title.
PS3558.03367F5   1991   90-37403
811'.54—dc20   CIP
                                                                AC

CURR.
PS
3558
.03367
F5
1991

CURR
PZ
7
.H66
Fin
1991

To my great-niece, Emma Ledbetter

—M.A.H.

For my children, David and Yona,
And for Leonard, whose love has been sustaining

—M.Z.

M. ZELDIS. 89.

THE SPLENDID LION

The splendid lion in repose
Has perky ears and button nose
And excellent mustachios
      Go *GRRR* for the lion!

He lies there perfectly at ease
Among the mossy jungle trees
With little freckles on his knees
      Go *GROWL* for the lion!

He looks like a big pussycat
But please beware before you pat
And do not dare to tell him "Scat"
      Go *SNARL* for the lion!

He has his mane, he has his might
He has a healthy appetite
Which often urges him to bite
      Go *ROAR* for the lion!

ABRACADABRA

Abracadabra
   The zebra is black
Abracadabra
   The zebra is white
Abracadabra
   The zebra is dark
Abracadabra
   The zebra is light

   Is it black striped with white?
   Is it white striped with black?
   Is it striped from the front?
   Is it striped from the back?

Abracadabra
   It's ink over snow
Abracadabra
   It's snow over ink
Abracadabra
   Does anyone know?
Abracadabra
   What do you think?

SOME SAY

Some say the donkey's grumpy
Some say the donkey's dumb
    They pile its back with bundles
    And scold it when it grumbles
    And thump it when it stumbles
No wonder it is glum!

Some say the donkey's stubborn
Some say it holds a grudge
    If I were so mistreated
    And got so overheated
    I'd threaten to be seated
And never *ever* budge!

EACH TIME THE WALRUS

Each time the walrus takes a walk
He really takes a waddle.
He flip-flops on his flipper tips
Which means he can't skedaddle.
But when the walrus takes a swim
The business is reversed.
If you were in a race with him
You wouldn't come in first.

M.ZELDIS 89.

SHEEP COUNTING

If you cannot fall asleep
    Why not try out counting sheep?
While you're lying in your bed
    Picture them inside your head
But as they wander through your mind
    Make sure they are the proper kind
If you picture them as white
    It's like turning on a light
When they're white, they're much too bright
    Make them all as black as night

ROUND AND ROUND

Round and round in loops of gold
The silent snake creeps up the hill
Behold its zigzag coils unfold
Perfectly moving
Yet perfectly still

A FINE FAT PIG

It feels so fine to be a pig
    So big and fat
    So fat and big

To wallow in the mud and muck
    What lucky fun
    What funny luck

To prance about on high-hooved heels
    Snort sniffs and snorts
    Squeal squeaks and squeals

    To dig and root
    To root and dig
It feels so fine to be a pig

ONE HALF OF THE GIRAFFE

One half
of the giraffe
is neck.
The other half
is not.
Now, necks
that are
a half of you
are really
quite a lot.

Although they let you
see afar
they're also
clearly spotted
(and even more
conspicuous
when they are
polka-dotted).

HOW ELEGANT THE ELEPHANT

How elegant the elephant
How mighty yet how mild
How elegant its mighty mate
How elegant its child
How toothsome are its ivory tusks
How luminous its eyes
How supple are its floppy ears
How jumbo is its size
How flexible its pudgy knees
How delicate its tail
But best of all
How nice its nose
Which works just like
A garden hose

YOO-HOO, MRS. KANGAROO!

Yoo-hoo, Mrs. Kangaroo!
How pleased your baby blue must be
Inside your pocket made of you!
Could you please make a place for me?

THE SPIDER'S WEB

The spider's web is where it lives
And traps unwary relatives.
The gnat and moth, the flea and fly,
Don't notice it as they flit by.
But if they're caught, they're two times stuck:
Both into lunch and out of luck.

IT'S FUN TO BE A FIRE DOG

It's fun to be a fire dog
    With ornamental spots
And live inside the firehouse
    And go to fires—lots!

I ride in fire engines
    With sirens at full blast
And everybody waves at me
    As I go flying past.

I enter burning buildings
    And rescue tiny tots.
It's fun to be a fire dog
    And go to fires—lots!

ONE TWO

A ram has got two
And a bull has got two
And a steer has got two
And a deer has got two
And a goat has got two
And a ewe has two, too
And a cow that goes moo
And an owl that goes whoo
  But the rhino has only got one
  Poor thing
  The rhino has only got one

A stag has got two
And a moose has got two
And an ox has got two
And an elk has got two
An impala has two
And an antelope, too
And the graceful gazelle
And the eland as well
  But the rhino has only got one
  Poor thing
  The rhino has only got one

Springboks and roebucks have two, they do
Chamois and oryx have two, they do
The bison has two
And so does the gnu
And the buffalo, too
And the yak in the zoo
And the grand caribou
And the great big kudu
  But the rhino has only got one
  Boo hoo
  The rhino has only got one

M. ZELDIS 89.

So many kinds of animals
So many shapes and sizes
So many funny spots and dots
So many strange disguises

So many hides and feathers
So many wools and furs
So many sorts of tweets and snorts
So many growls and purrs

So many shades and colors
So many stripes and blends
So many kinds from olden times
So many brand-new friends

Mary Ann Hoberman was born in Stamford, Connecticut, and received a B.A. and M.A. from Smith College and an M.A. from Yale University. She is the author of many books for children, including the award-winning A HOUSE IS A HOUSE FOR ME, illustrated by Betty Fraser.

Ms. Hoberman lives in Greenwich, Connecticut, with her husband, an architect and artist.

Malcah Zeldis was born in New York City and grew up in Detroit, Michigan. Her folk paintings have been included in over seventy group exhibits and seven one-woman shows. Her artwork is in the permanent collections of many museums around the world, including the Museum of American Folk Art, the Jewish Museum, the Milwaukee Museum of Art, the Musée d'Art Naif de l'Île-de-France, and the Smithsonian Institution, among others.